FIRST AMERICANS
The Cherokee

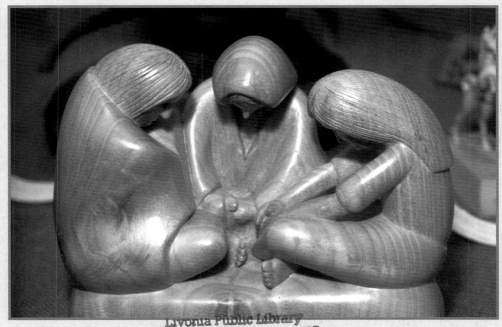

SARAH De CAPUA

 **Marshall Cavendish**
Benchmark
New York

ACKNOWLEDGMENTS

Series consultant: Raymond Bial

Benchmark Books
Marshall Cavendish
99 White Plains Road
Tarrytown, New York 10591
www.marshallcavendish.us

Text copyright © 2006 by Marshall Cavendish Corporation
Map and illustrations copyright © 2006 by Marshall Cavendish Corporation

Library of Congress Cataloging-in-Publication Data
De Capua, Sarah.
The Cherokee / by Sarah De Capua.
p. cm. -- (First Americans)
Includes bibliographical references and index.
ISBN 0-7614-1895-4
1. Cherokee Indians--History--Juvenile literature. 2. Cherokee Indians--Social life and customs--Juvenile literature. I. Title. II.
Series: First Americans (Marshall Cavendish Benchmark)
E99.C5D4 2005
975.004'97557--dc22
2004027573

On the cover: A Cherokee from the town of Cherokee, North Carolina, prepares for a ceremonial dance.
Title page: A wood carving by a Cherokee artist
Photo Research by Joan Meisel

Cover photo: Kevin Fleming/Corbis

Corbis 10; Bettmann, 6; Jay Dickman, 28; Kevin Fleming, 31; Richard A. Cooke, 32, 38. *Nativestock.com*: Marilyn "Angel" Wynn, 1, 4, 13, 14, 16, 17, 18, 20, 21 (left & right), 22, 33, 34, 36. *Peter Arnold, Inc.*: Clyde H. Smith, 7, 23; Johann Schumacher, 30. *The Philbrook Museum of Art*, Tulsa, Oklahoma: *Great Spirit Sends His Helpers to Guide Man to the Land Beyond*, Donald Vann, 1970, watercolor on laid paper (upon poster board), Gift of Phillips Petroleum Company, 1995.7.104, 26.

Map by Christopher Santoro
Series design by Symon Chow

Printed in China
1 3 5 6 4 2

CONTENTS

1 · WHO ARE THE CHEROKEE PEOPLE?

The Cherokee Nation is the largest Native American tribe in the United States and Canada. They number more than three hundred thousand. The Cherokee once lived and hunted in the Blue Ridge and Great Smoky mountains, a large area of land in the present-day states of Virginia, Tennessee, North Carolina, South Carolina, Georgia, and Alabama. The mountains get their names from the blue-gray haze that floats over their peaks. The first Cherokee capital was *Tanasi*. The name of the state of Tennessee comes from this Cherokee town.

Throughout their history, the Cherokee have called themselves *Ani Yunwiya*, which means "principle people." Today, most Cherokee live in northeastern Oklahoma. A smaller number live on a **reservation** in North Carolina.

A Cherokee man dressed in traditional clothing for a special celebration.

Hernando de Soto and his army met the Cherokee in 1540. The Spanish came to North America to search for gold.

The first contact between the Cherokee and Europeans occurred in 1540 when Spanish explorer Hernando de Soto arrived with his army. The Spanish were searching for gold, but didn't find any. Around 1690, Cornelius Dougherty, an Irishman from Virginia, became the first white trader to live among the Cherokee. English traders were soon common among the Cherokee.

The Blue Ridge Mountains, where the Cherokee first lived.

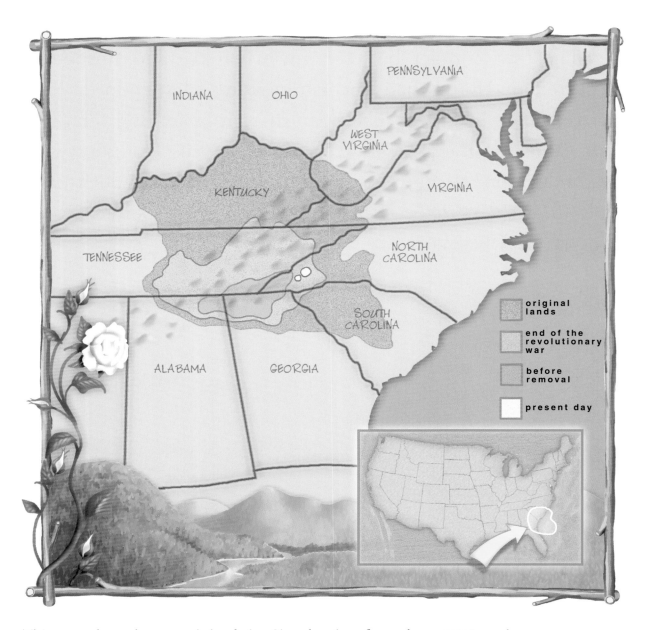

This map shows how much land the Cherokee lost from about 1775 to the present.

By the 1700s, the Cherokee, who were often at war with other tribes, were fighting the European settlers. In the French and Indian War (1754–1763), the Cherokee fought with the French against the British. When the British won the war, they took land away from the Cherokee.

During the American Revolution (1775–1783), the Cherokee fought on the side of Britain. After the colonists won the war, the United States government claimed Cherokee lands as their own.

The War of 1812 (1812–1814) was fought between the British and Americans. The Cherokee sided with the Americans. In 1814 General Andrew Jackson led an army that included many Cherokee warriors to victory at Horseshoe Bend, in present-day southern Alabama.

In 1829 gold was found on Cherokee lands in what is now northeast Georgia. Americans arrived from all over looking for more. The state of Georgia seized the land from the Cherokee. While the U.S. Supreme Court ruled that the Cherokees' lands could not be taken from them, the Georgia

state government ignored the ruling. Cherokee houses, farms, animals, and crops were taken away.

Then, in 1830, Congress passed the Indian Removal Act. President Andrew Jackson, who had led the army that included Cherokee to victory in the War of 1812, signed it into law. Under this law, all Indians living east of the Mississippi River were to be moved to new lands in the West. The law also created Indian Territory in what is now the state of

John Ross, principal chief of the Cherokee from 1828 to 1866.

Oklahoma. The Indian Removal Act resulted in the forced removal of the Cherokee, Chickasaw, Choctaw, Creek, and Seminole—known as the "five civilized tribes"—from their lands.

In 1838 sixteen thousand Cherokee were forced off their lands and made to travel seven hundred miles, many on foot, through sleet and snow. The Cherokee called this journey "the trail where they cried." Today it is called the Trail of Tears.

A small group of Cherokee escaped the forced march west. **Descendants** of this group living in North Carolina are today known as the Eastern Band of Cherokee.

Quatie Ross on the Trail of Tears

Quatie Ross, wife of Chief John Ross, traveled the Trail of Tears from north Georgia. She described the journey in her own words:

Long time we travel on way to new land. People feel bad when they leave Old Nation. Women cry and make sad wails. Children cry and many men cry. But they say nothing and just put their heads down and keep going toward West. Many days pass and people die very much.

Legend says that Quatie Ross had a cold, but gave her only blanket to a child. She died of pneumonia at Little Rock, Arkansas, in 1839. She never reached Indian Territory.

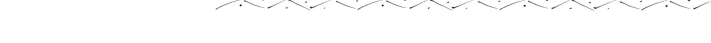

Throughout Cherokee history, families have lived together in groups called **clans**. A Cherokee clan is a group of families who are related through the mother. Each clan is led by a woman. The Cherokee have seven clans: Bird, Blue, Deer, Long Hair, Paint, Wild Potato, and Wolf.

Long ago, the Cherokee lived in towns made up of about fifty houses. The town was surrounded by a fence for protection. The Cherokee lived in two kinds of houses. In summer, they lived in houses made of wood or logs. In winter, they moved into small, round houses called *asi* (oh-SEE). These houses had a pit in the center for fires. Built close to the ground, the heat from the fire kept the family warm. After the Europeans arrived, the Cherokee began to live in log cabins, and sometimes brick houses, all year.

This museum exhibit shows how the Cherokee lived before the arrival of European explorers.

Cherokee life revolved around farming. They grew corn, beans, squash, sweet potatoes, and tobacco. Women gathered wild berries, nuts, and fruits. Men hunted deer, bear, and elk. Children were taught to respect adults. Boys learned how to hunt and be warriors. Girls learned household chores, gardening, cooking, and making clothing.

Cherokee government was the same in every town. It was

Early Cherokee houses had thick, clay-covered walls and no windows.

based on the clan system. Each town had two chiefs. The peace chief wore a white headdress. The peace chief was the leader when the town was at peace. The war chief wore a red headdress and was the leader when the town was at war. Both chiefs were members of the town council. The town council met in a large building that stood in the center of every town. The building was called a council house.

The Cherokee learned to make log homes when English settlers came in the 1700s.

Sequoyah

Sequoyah was born around 1770. He was the son of a Cherokee mother and an English father. He wanted to help the Cherokee learn to read and write. From 1809 to 1821 he worked to develop a system of writing the Cherokee language. He made up a system using symbols to represent different speech sounds, called a **syllabary**, of eighty-six characters. The Cherokee Nation officially adopted Sequoyah's syllabary in 1821. It was the first written Indian language in North America.

The syllabary worked liked an alphabet. But each symbol stood for a sound in the Cherokee language. The Cherokee did not have to learn to spell because the symbols stood for sounds, not letters.

In 1828 Sequoyah helped to start the *Cherokee Phoenix*. It was the first Cherokee newspaper, and the first American Indian newspaper. It would not have been possible without Sequoyah's syllabary.

The town council was made up of seven well-respected elders. One elder represented each clan. There was also a Council of Beloved Women. One woman from each clan sat on this council. The councils worked to solve everyday Cherokee problems.

Cherokee clothing was very practical. Men wore a gar-

A Cherokee council house, where the town council met to discuss and solve the community's problems.

ment called a breechclout. It was made of soft deerskin. A man would tie a piece of leather around his waist like a belt. One end of the breechclout was brought up under the belt in front. The other end was tucked under the belt in back. While hunting, men wore deerskin moccasins. Men sometimes wore deerskin leggings that protected their legs from cuts and

This Cherokee man (left) and woman (right) are wearing the traditional dress of their people.

scratches when they walked through wooded areas. In winter, men wore long deerskin hunting shirts or cloaks made of wild turkey feathers or animal fur. Fur cloaks were worn with the fur on the inside for warmth.

Women usually wore deerskin skirts that wrapped around

This illustration shows how Cherokee clothing changed after the arrival of Europeans in North America. The Cherokee began to make clothes from cloth and blankets.

their waists. The skirts reached to just above the knees. In town, women went barefoot, like the men. They wore moccasins in winter, however. For both men and women, winter moccasins covered the leg almost to the knee. In cold weather, women wore dresses that hung from one shoulder. The other shoulder was bare.

Beadwork is one of the traditional Cherokee crafts that is still practiced today.

Bean Bread

This is a modern recipe for a very old Cherokee food. Ask an adult to help you make the following recipe. Always wash your hands with soap and water before you begin.

Ingredients:
- 1 cup cornmeal
- 1/2 cup flour
- 2 teaspoons baking powder
- 1 tablespoon sugar
- 2 cups milk
- 1/4 cup shortening, melted and cooled
- 1 egg, beaten
- 2 tablespoons honey
- 4 cups brown beans, drained

Preheat oven to 450 degrees Fahrenheit. Grease an 8-by-8 inch square pan. In a large bowl, mix all ingredients except the beans. Gently fold the beans into the batter. Pour batter into the pan. Bake about 30 minutes, just until the top browns.

After the arrival of Europeans, the Cherokee began to make clothes from the cloth they received in trade. They also traded for the Europeans' wool blankets, which they often made into winter coats.

Aside from the foods they grew on farms and the animals hunted for meat, the Cherokee also ate fish. Cherokee men fished in rivers and streams with spears and nets. Cherokee who lived near the coast caught herring, sturgeon, and turtles. They used fishhooks made from animal bone. On beaches, they collected clams, mussels, and oysters.

Traditionally, the Cherokee were very religious. They prayed to spirits often. The Cherokee believed that every living thing had a spirit made by the Creator. They believed that the Creator used the spirits of animals, birds, or plants to bring them messages. The Cherokee also believed their dreams contained messages from the spirits.

The Cherokee name for the Creator means "the Elder Fires Above." There were three parts to the Creator. In Cherokee, the names for each mean, "head of all power," "place of uniting," and "place below the breast." Later, Christian missionaries told the Cherokee about the Father, Son, and Holy Spirit. This fit with what the Cherokee already believed. This may be one reason the Cherokee accepted Christianity. Today, many Cherokee believe in both their traditional religion and Christianity.

In this painting by a Cherokee artist, the Great Spirit sends his helper to guide the Cherokee to the Land Beyond.

HOW THE EARTH WAS MADE

Long ago, there was nothing but water covering the world. All the animals lived above Sky Rock, which the Cherokee called *Galun'lati*. It was very crowded there. So the animals decided to send one of their own down to find out what was under the water.

A little water beetle volunteered to go. It searched over the water, but couldn't find dry land. Then it dived to the bottom and came back with a little bit of mud. The mud grew and spread until it became Earth. It floated on the water and was held up by four cords. The cords—north, south, east, and west—were attached to Sky Rock.

At first the Earth was flat. The ground was wet. The animals sent different birds down to see if it was dry yet. None could find dry land. Finally, the great buzzard flew down, looking for a place where the animals could live. He flew very low all over the Earth. When he reached what became Cherokee country, he was very tired. His wings began to beat against the soft ground. Wherever his wings hit the Earth, a valley formed. Where his wings turned up again, mountains were made. The animals did not want the whole Earth to become mountains, so they called the great buzzard back. That is why the Cherokee country is full of mountains.

Ceremonies were an important part of Cherokee life. The ceremonies often included music and dancing. Some ceremonies were held to celebrate the change of seasons.

The most important ceremony of the year was the Green Corn Ceremony. This was celebrated when the corn was ripe, usually in July or August. It was held to thank the Creator for the harvest. The Green Corn Ceremony also marked the start

The Cherokee believed that everything in the natural world had a spirit.

of the Cherokee new year. Today, the Cherokee still perform the Green Corn Ceremony.

When important visitors arrived in a Cherokee town, the Eagle Dance was performed to welcome them.

Another Cherokee ceremony was called the Booger Dance. It was used to make fun of Cherokee enemies, such as warriors from other tribes. The dancers wore masks made

Cherokee dancers perform a traditional ceremonial dance.

A Cherokee Booger Dance mask

from wood or **gourds**.

Masks were also used in dances performed before a hunting trip. The masks stood for deer, bear, and buffalo. The Cherokee believed that these masks would make hunting easier.

The Cherokee marriage ceremony took place around the sacred fire in the council house. The bride and groom were separately covered with blue blankets. They and their guests were blessed by the Cherokee priest or priestess. Cherokee songs were sung. When the couple was declared to be married, the priest or priestess removed the blue blankets and covered them both with one white blanket. This meant their new life together had begun. Cherokee couples did not exchange rings, but food. The groom gave the bride **venison**. This meant he would provide for their family. The bride gave the groom corn to show she could take care of their family. Following the ceremony, the couple and the entire

Feather dance wands are used in Cherokee ceremonial dances to keep time with the music.

town celebrated with a feast that included food, singing, and joyous dancing.

When a baby was born, townspeople would ask, "Is it a *bow* (boy) or a *sifter* (girl)?" This question reflected the traditional roles of Cherokee boys and girls. One or two days after birth, the Cherokee priest or priestess would wave the baby four times over a sacred fire while saying a blessing. On the fourth or seventh day after birth, the priest or priestess took

At some celebrations, Cherokee women wore tortoise shell leg rattles like these on their lower legs as they danced. The sounds the rattles made added to the music.

the baby to a river and prayed that he or she would enjoy a long, happy life. Afterward, the naming ceremony was held. The most respected older woman in the community named the baby. She was known as Beloved Woman.

When a Cherokee died, a close male relative, such as a son, closed the person's eyelids and washed the body with water or a mixture made with boiled willow root. The town's priest or priestess buried the dead. The body was buried either in the floor under the place where the person died, under the home's fire pit, or outside near the house. A chief was buried under his seat in the council house. The Cherokee believed in an afterlife. The soul went to live either with the Divine Beings or to the Place of Bad Spirits, depending on the kind of life the person lived.

4 · A CHANGING WORLD

In the United States today, there are three groups of Cherokee. The largest band is known as the Cherokee Nation in Oklahoma. The United Keetoowah Band also lives in Oklahoma. The Eastern Band of Cherokee lives in North Carolina. The Cherokee Nation and the United Keetoowah Band each owns the land they live on. Only the Eastern Band lives on a reservation. Each band is made up of a principal chief and a tribal council. Together, they run the tribe's government, as well as schools and social programs.

Today's Cherokee mix their traditional ways with the modern American lifestyle. They live in homes much like those of many Americans. They wear the same kind of clothing, too. But they still honor Cherokee traditions whenever

The Qualla Boundary Reservation of the Eastern Band of Cherokee in Cherokee, North Carolina, is tucked away in the Smoky Mountains.

they can. The old ways are taught to the young by their elders. The Cherokee, young and old, participate in **powwows**, dances, and tribal celebrations.

While some Cherokee work as cattle ranchers, others work as poultry farmers. Some work as traditional artists. They make and sell Cherokee baskets, pottery, and jewelry. Others make their living as doctors, lawyers, teachers, police officers, or firefighters. Some serve the United States in the military.

These Cherokee women keep their traditions alive by making baskets the way their ancestors did.

Cherokee, North Carolina, is the capital of the Eastern Band of Cherokee. The reservation is called Qualla Boundary. Additional tribal lands are found at the Snowbird community near Robbinsville and in Cherokee County, North Carolina. The Cherokee of Qualla Boundary maintain a living history center where visitors can explore Cherokee traditions and practices.

Today's Cherokee have succeeded in the modern world. But their history and traditions remain deeply important to them.

TIME LINE

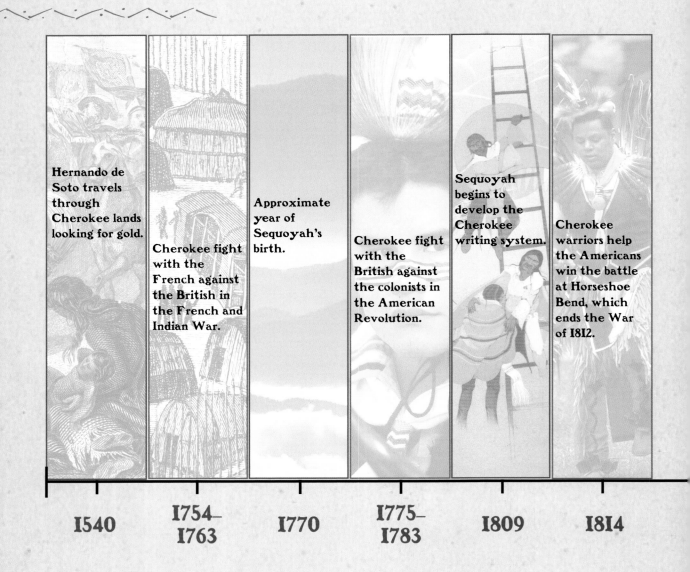

Hernando de Soto travels through Cherokee lands looking for gold.

Cherokee fight with the French against the British in the French and Indian War.

Approximate year of Sequoyah's birth.

Cherokee fight with the British against the colonists in the American Revolution.

Sequoyah begins to develop the Cherokee writing system.

Cherokee warriors help the Americans win the battle at Horseshoe Bend, which ends the War of 1812.

1540

1754–1763

1770

1775–1783

1809

1814

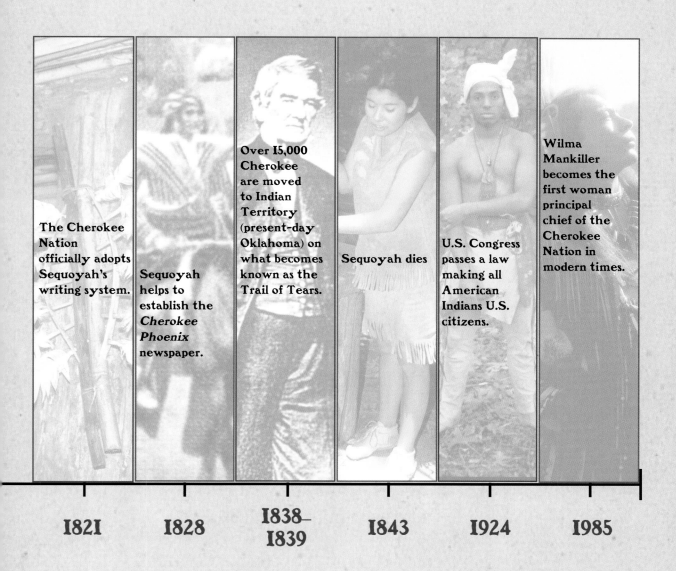

The Cherokee Nation officially adopts Sequoyah's writing system.

Sequoyah helps to establish the *Cherokee Phoenix* newspaper.

Over 15,000 Cherokee are moved to Indian Territory (present-day Oklahoma) on what becomes known as the Trail of Tears.

Sequoyah dies

U.S. Congress passes a law making all American Indians U.S. citizens.

Wilma Mankiller becomes the first woman principal chief of the Cherokee Nation in modern times.

1821

1828

1838–1839

1843

1924

1985

GLOSSARY

clan: A group of people related to a common ancestor.

descendants: The children, grandchildren, and so on of people who lived long ago.

gourds: Fruits with a rounded shape similar to that of a squash or pumpkin. Gourds are sometimes used for decorations and to make crafts, bowls, or jugs.

powwow: A gathering where Native Americans celebrate their heritage.

reservation: An area of land set aside by the U.S. government for use by American Indians.

syllabary: A table of symbols that stand for syllables (speech sounds) instead of letters.

venison: The meat of an animal, usually deer.

FIND OUT MORE

Books

Bial, Raymond. *The Cherokee*. NY: Marshall Cavendish, 1999.

Fitterer, C. Ann. *Sequoyah: Native American Scholar*. Chanhassen, MN: The Child's World, 2003.

Gunderson, Mary. *American Indian Cooking Before 1500*. Mankato, MN: Blue Earth Books, 2001.

Press, Petra. *The Cherokee*. Mankato, MN: Compass Point Books, 2002.

Santella, Andrew. *The Cherokee*. Danbury, CT: Children's Press, 2001.

Web Sites

Cherokee Heritage Center in Tahlequah, Oklahoma.
www.cherokeeheritage.org

Museum of the Cherokee Indian, in Cherokee, North Carolina
www.cherokeemuseum.org

Official Cherokee Nation Web Site
www.cherokee.org

Sequoyah Birthplace Museum
www.sequoyahmuseum.org

Trail of Tears National Historic Trail
www.nps.gov/trte

About the Author

Sarah De Capua is the author of many books, including biographies, and geography and history titles. She has always been fascinated by the earliest inhabitants of North America. In this series, the author has also written *The Iroquois*. Born and raised in Connecticut, Ms. De Capua now calls Colorado home.